JELLYFISH

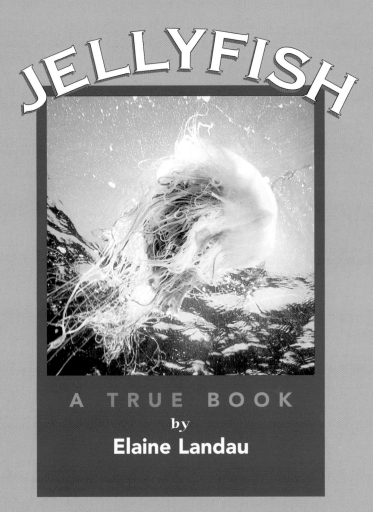

A TRUE BOOK

by

Elaine Landau

Children's Press®
A Division of Grolier Publishing
New York London Hong Kong Sydney
Danbury, Connecticut

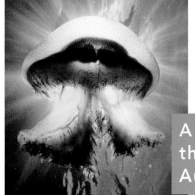

Reading Consultant
Linda Cornwell
Learning Resource Consultant
Indiana Department
of Education

A jellyfish in
the waters of
Australia

Library of Congress Cataloging-in-Publication Data

Landau, Elaine.
    Jellyfish / by Elaine Landau.
        p.   cm. — (A true book)
    Includes bibliographical references and index.
    Summary: Introduces the size, shape, colors, and stinging tentacles of
jellyfish and examines their survival in the world's waters since before the
age of the dinosaurs.
    ISBN: 0-516-20676-1 (lib. bdg.)   0-516-26494-X (pbk.)
    1. Jellyfishes—Juvenile literature.   [1. Jellyfishes.]   I. Title.   II. Series.
QL377.S4L35   1999
593.5`3—dc21   98-16116
                                                                                          CIP
                                                                                          AC

Contents

Jellyfish come in a variety of shapes, sizes, and colors.

An Unusual Sea Animal

What sea creature is called a fish, but is not really a fish at all? The answer is a jellyfish.

Jellyfish are strange-looking sea animals found in every ocean of the world. They are also found in some freshwater lakes and ponds. They are probably not a bit like the

Jellyfish are found in oceans (above) and lakes (right).

animals you are used to seeing or hearing about. Jellyfish range in size from less than 1 inch (3 centimeters) across to about 7 feet (2 meters).

Jellyfish have no brains, no hearts, and no bones. Yet they have lived in the waters of the world for more than 650 million years. Long before dinosaurs roamed Earth, jellyfish floated in the seas.

A diver encounters a giant jellyfish.

Jellyfish

A jellyfish is right at home in
the ocean because it has a
body that is made up almost
completely of water. The jellylike material that makes up its
body is held together by two
layers of cells. Its watery habitat provides the additional
support the jellyfish needs to

Jellyfish (left) are perfectly suited to their watery habitat. This jellyfish (below) has washed up on the beach.

live and travel with ease. If a jellyfish is taken out of the water, it quickly dries up and dies.

Here, you can clearly see the upside-down bowl shape of the jellyfish.

What makes a jellyfish look so interesting is its bell-shaped body. Some people say it looks like an upside-down bowl or an open umbrella. These bell-shaped animals come in many colors—lavender, pink, blue, orange, and different combinations of colors.

Jellyfish that tend to stay near the sunlight at the water's surface are often colorless. But those that swim in deeper waters can be red or purple.

Jellyfish range in color from colorless (left) to purple (right).

Hanging down from the rim of the jellyfish's bell-shaped body are its dangling tentacles. The number and length of the tentacles depend on the type of jellyfish. But the tentacles usually contain many stinging cells.

The length of a jellyfish's tentacles can range from a few inches (right) to several feet (far right).

This photograph is a close-up of the oral arms of a moon jellyfish. (Note the tiny fish stuck inside.)

A short tube that hangs down from the center of the jellyfish's body is its mouth and digestive tube. In some jellyfish, this central tube is surrounded by frilly jelly

The oral arms of a sea nettle jellyfish look like curly ribbon.

pieces called oral arms, or mouth arms. They look like curly ribbons in the water.

Jellyfish have no eyes, but they do have sense organs called eye spots. These eye spots are part of a nerve cell network in the jellyfish's body that helps it to find food and detect danger. This simple system of senses tells the jellyfish whether it is headed up toward the water's surface or down into the deep sea.

Is It A Jellyfish?

The Portuguese man-of-war looks like a jellyfish, but isn't one. It's a jellylike animal found in warm

water seas throughout the world. The Portuguese man-of-war has a gas-filled balloonlike float. Many long tentacles dangle from it. The tentacles on some of these animals can stretch as long as 100 feet (30 m) or more. Each tentacle contains thousands of stinging cells.

The Portuguese man-of-war uses these stinging cells to paralyze its prey, or food.

Hundreds, or even thousands, of these floating creatures are sometimes spotted in groups. Often their long tentacles become tangled in fishermen's lines. But people fishing or swimming should try to avoid the Portuguese man-of-war. It can deliver a painful sting that may result in serious side effects. These include a severe rash, painful welts, fever, or difficulty breathing.

You can recognize a Portuguese man-of-war by its float that rests on the water's surface.

People should stay a safe distance away from the Portuguese man-of-war.

Riders On the Tide

Jellyfish are drifters. This means that they go where the water's current takes them. Jellyfish usually travel in fairly large groups. But sometimes one or two jellyfish drift about on their own.

Although some jellyfish are quite large, their bodies are

Swimmers sometimes encounter large groups of jellyfish.

A jellyfish floats the ocean's current.

light in the water. This makes it easy for them to ride with the current's flow. However, they are not completely at the mercy of the winds and the waves. They can control their movements a little with their own style of

This jellyfish is propelling itself through the waters of the Indian Ocean.

swimming. A jellyfish swims by spreading open its umbrellalike body and then quickly pulling it shut again. This pulsing movement pushes the water out from under its body and propels the creature along.

Besides swimming short distances through the sea, many jellyfish swim up toward the water's surface at night to look for food. During the day, they stay away from the bright sunlight by sinking deeper into the sea. However, some types of jellyfish like sunlight and bask in it whenever possible.

Jellyfish are well protected in their watery world. Even the colorful kinds of jellyfish are transparent, or clear like glass. This quality makes them diffi-

A jellyfish floats in the sunlight near the water's surface (left). It can be difficult to spot some kinds of jellyfish because they are transparent (above).

cult to see in the water. That gives them some defense from enemies because jellyfish have few places to hide.

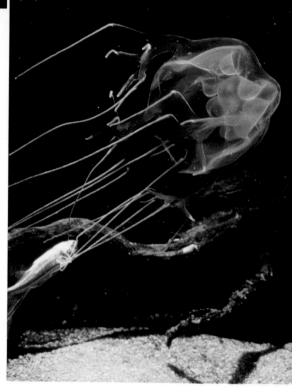

In this photograph (above), a young jellyfish (left) feeds on another kind of jellyfish in a tropical lake. This jellyfish (right) has spread its tentacles to capture a small fish for food.

Jellyfish do not have to go too far to find a meal. They live on many of the other creatures that ride the water's tides. They simply trap and eat whatever drifts by in the water, including young fish, small water animals, and even other jellyfish.

To catch its food, a jellyfish spreads out its tentacles. As soon as its prey (the animal that is to be eaten) brushes past, the tentacles' stinging cells go to work. The cells thrust stingers into the victim. These stingers deliver a poison that either paralyzes or kills the prey. Then the jellyfish draws in its tentacles and brings the food to its mouth tube.

Small fish sometimes live beneath the bells of some large jellyfish. The jellyfish's stinging tentacles protect the fish from predators. The fish keep from being stung themselves by staying away from the

A close-up
of a fish
meal stuck
in a jelly-
fish's
tentacles

dangerous tentacles that sur-
round them. At one time, people believed that these fish
were not affected by the jellyfish's sting. But this is not true.
If these small fish accidentally
swim up against a tentacle,
they become a fish dinner!

In some cases, crabs have been seen hitching a ride on a jellyfish. The hard, outer shell of the crab protects it from the jellyfish's sting. And besides finding a method of transportation, the crabs usually catch a little of the food the jellyfish traps.

Some jellyfish have been known to sting swimmers and divers. A single sting can make a person's skin burn and itch. In more severe cases, a painful red welt, or raised mark, may result. Some victims have

Although this snorkeler is swimming in a lake full of stingless jellyfish, contact with most jellyfish should be avoided.

experienced difficulty in breathing. The sting of certain types of jellyfish can even cause death.

Among the most dangerous jellyfish is the Australian sea wasp. This jellyfish is found along the northeast coast of Australia and the Philippines. It is colorless and has a box-shaped bell body. Although the Australian sea wasp is only about 5 inches (13 cm) across, its tentacles can extend almost 40 inches (102 cm). These

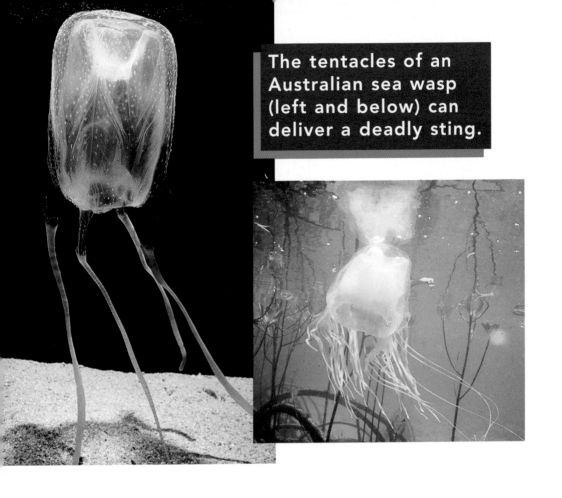

The tentacles of an Australian sea wasp (left and below) can deliver a deadly sting.

jellyfish prefer shallow water and are often found near bays. An Australian sea wasp can kill anyone who touches it within a few minutes.

The Lion's mane jellyfish

Though not as deadly, another jellyfish that delivers a powerful sting is the Lion's mane. This jellyfish is almost 7 feet (2 meters) across. Its tentacles reach 100 feet (30 m) long. Its bell varies in color from pale pink to golden red or purple. Its oral arms are usually violet and its tentacles may be either yellow or red.

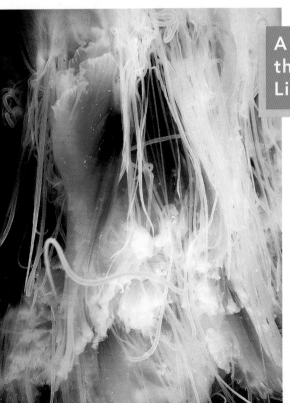

A close-up view of the tentacles of a Lion's mane jellyfish

The Lion's mane is found in the coolest regions of the Atlantic and the Pacific oceans, as well as in the Arctic Ocean. It also lives in the Baltic Sea and the waters surrounding parts of Alaska, Japan, and China.

Although some jellyfish are dangerous to humans, many are completely harmless. However, it is always wise to steer clear of jellyfish. Don't be tempted to touch the long tentacles trailing from this unique sea creature. If a jelly-fish is swimming with its tentacles spread, it is looking for food. You don't want to be mistaken for a meal!

If you are swimming near jellyfish, don't try to reach out and touch them.

What If A Jellyfish Stings You?

Don't panic if you are stung by a jellyfish. If the animal's tentacles have stuck to your skin, use a thick glove, cloth, or towel to pull them off. Never touch the tentacles with your bare hands. A tentacle can still sting you even if it's separated from the rest of the animal's body. Wash the injury thoroughly and apply vinegar to the sting area. You may want to see a doctor to be sure you don't have an allergic reaction to the jellyfish sting.

Beaches are common place encounter jellyfis

The sting of these thimble jellyfish can cause severe rashes and painful itching.

More Jellyfish

Jellyfish reproduce, or multiply, in an unusual way. Like many other sea creatures, the female's eggs are fertilized by the male's sperm. But then the young they produce begin a process that might seem strange. These young, called larvae, attach themselves to a

Tiny jellyfish, called medusoids, later become polyps.

solid surface, such as a rocky
ledge or an underwater cave.
Then they develop into polyps.
During this stage of its life
cycle, the polyp does more

than just grow. It also clones itself, or makes an exact copy. Through a process called budding, a single polyp divides to form many identical polyps.

Two jellyfish in their polyp stage

An adult jelly-fish formed after passing through its polyp stage

The newly formed polyps soon split off and swim away on their own. These young jelly-fish eventually grow into adult jellyfish. And the life cycle begins again with fertilization.

Ancient Survivors

The jellyfish's huge underwater world covers much of our planet. For millions of years, these sea creatures have survived great changes in the water's density (thickness), temperature, and saltiness. They have carved out a place for themselves in Earth's waters.

41

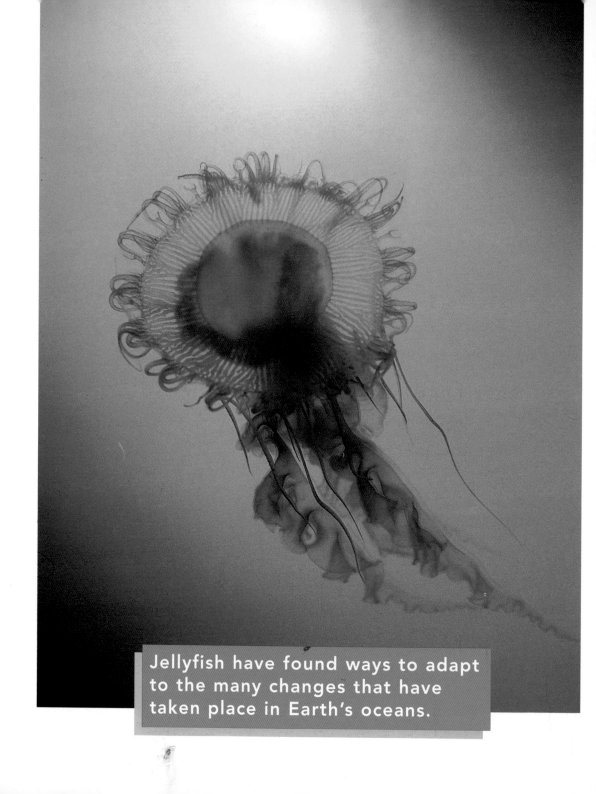

Jellyfish have found ways to adapt to the many changes that have taken place in Earth's oceans.

As long as the world has plenty of water, jellyfish will probably survive.

Jellyfish have been found in waters as deep as 3,200 feet (1,000 m). Perfectly suited to their surroundings, they are likely to be with us for millions of years to come.

To Find Out More

Here are some additional resources to help you learn more about jellyfish and the ocean:

Books

Brenner, Barbara and Bernice Chardiet. **Where's That Fish?** Scholastic, 1994.

Davis, Gary. **Coral Reef.** Children's Press, 1997.

Hahn, Mary D. **Jellyfish Season.** Avon, 1992.

Kovacs, Deborah and Kate Madin. **Beneath Blue Waters: Meetings With Remarkable Deep-Sea Creatures.** Viking, 1996.

Stone, Lynn M. **Jellyfish.** Rourke Corporation, 1993.

Organizations and Online Sites

Jellyfish
http://www.encarta.msn. com/index/concise/0V0L08

From the Encarta Concise Encyclopedia, this site is a brief introduction to jelly-fish, with pictures and links to other sites.

Jellyfish
http://www.eagle.online. discovery.com/area/nature/ jellyfish/slides

Sponsored by the Discovery Channel Online, this site offers fascinating close-up photographs of several different kinds of jellyfish.

Jellyfish Trivia
http://www.aqua.org/ animals/species/jellies/ trivia.html

This site, sponsored by the National Aquarium in Baltimore, Maryland, is a jellyfish trivia test.

Ocean Animals
www.mobot.org/MBGnet/ salt/animals/index.htm

This Yahooligans!™ site is full of pictures and informa-tion about the many kinds of animals that live in the world's oceans.

Ocean Society
441 Ridgewater Drive
Marietta, GA   30068

Important Words

bask to lie in the sunshine

budding process through which a single jellyfish polyp divides to form many new identical polyps

detect to find or to discover

fertilize to make able to reproduce

habitat environment in which an animal usually lives

predator an animal that eats other animals

propel to move forward

transparent clear like glass

Index

Meet the Author

Elaine Landau has a Bachelor of Arts degree in English and Journalism from New York University and a Masters degree in Library and Information Science from Pratt Institute. She has worked as a newspaper reporter, children's book editor, and a youth services librarian, but especially enjoys writing for young people.

Ms. Landau has written more than one hundred nonfiction books on various topics. She lives in Miami, Florida, with her husband, Norman, and son, Michael.